SILENT IN FINISTERRE

Jane Griffiths was born in Exeter in 1970, and brought up in Devon and Holland. After reading English at Oxford, where her poem 'The House' won the Newdigate Prize, she worked as a book-binder in London and Norfolk. Returning to Oxford, she completed her doctorate on the Tudor poet John Skelton and worked on the Oxford English Dictionary for two years. After teaching English Literature at St Edmund Hall, Oxford, and then at the universities of Edinburgh and Bristol, she now teaches at Wadham College, Oxford. She won an Eric Gregory Award for her poetry in 1996. Her book *Another Country: New & Selected Poems* (Bloodaxe Books, 2008), which included a new collection, *Eclogue Over Merlin Street* (2008), together with large selections from her previous two Bloodaxe collections, *A Grip on Thin Air* (2000) and *Icarus on Earth* (2005), was shortlisted for the Forward Prize for Best Collection. Her most recent collections from Bloodaxe are *Terrestrial Variations* (2012), and *Silent in Finisterre* (2017), which received a Poetry Book Society Recommendation.

JANE GRIFFITHS

Silent in Finisterre

BLOODAXE BOOKS

ISBN: 978 1 78037 356 0

First published 2017 by
Bloodaxe Books Ltd
Eastburn
South Park
Hexham
Northumberland NE46 1BS

www.bloodaxebooks.com
For further information about Bloodaxe titles
please visit our website or write to
the above address for a catalogue.

Supported using public funding by
ARTS COUNCIL
ENGLAND

Cover design: Neil Astley & Pamela Robertson-Pearce.

Printed in Great Britain by Bell & Bain Limited, Glasgow, Scotland, on
acid-free paper sourced from mills with FSC chain of custody certification.

Let a man get up and say, 'Behold, this is the truth,' and instantly I perceive a sandy cat filching a piece of fish in the background. Look, you have forgotten the cat, I say.

VIRGINIA WOOLF, *The Waves*

ACKNOWLEDGEMENTS

Acknowledgements are due to the editors of the following publications, in which some of these poems have appeared: *The Alhambra Poetry Calendar, The Golden Hour, The Oxford Magazine, Oxford Poetry, PN Review, The Poetry Review, The Rialto,* and *The Same.*

'Anonymous' was commissioned by Ian Starsmore as part of his installation of artworks involving ladders in Cambridge University Library in 2007.

I should also like to thank Polly Clark and Esther Morgan for reading earlier drafts of several of these poems and for their astute suggestions

CONTENTS

Lessons from My First Giraffe

(for Nigel and Hilary)

The habits of camouflage.
How to approach a mezzanine.
How to articulate at the knee delicately as a lady
                    stepping down from her carriage.
A preference for what's out of reach.
How to trust the improbable.
Vertigo, or a warped sense of perspective.
How to wink, slowly.
How to curl my lip to the shape of a leaf.
How to keep my feet on the ground in Gandy Street
while stretching my neck languidly to graze the long
slopes round Rougemont Castle where goldfish swim
star-like in the bowl of the hill.
A fondness for Marmite.
The fissure between the parts and the whole.

In the beginning

(for Peter)

In the beginning was the tree,
the hooked silhouette of it, the swing,
the inedible apples.

In the beginning was the train,
the rumour of it, its reverberations
quick between the branches.

In the beginning was the sun,
kaleidoscopic, held up for inspection
between finger and thumb.

And beyond the tree the world
was a solid circumference, a perfect
round of hills

where north was up the road
and the sea was down. There were three
gates to the garden

in the beginning, before the sun
set above the station and the tree blacked
into a sky

where at night the trains kept running
on and on and a voice called home
all the possible destinations.

Perspective

Her first view was buddleia and Bramley.
The sky was silk-skein and a long way off.

Its grass-and-dust smell blew with the wind,
which came and went. It was true north.

Her second was river, broad and industrious,
strong-arming barges and container freight.

It was here she dropped a small gold coin:
knew it lost, but *lost somewhere in the world.*

In her mind's eye it was centred, like a pupil.

Her third view was building site, a dream
of brick repeating brick. It was treelessness

and puddle. Its smell of mud persisted.
She could make head nor tail of it,

though there was skating, some months,
and each spring, marbles: hoards of them,

circled on their still-stopped lava flows,
lost and won in pockets of the earth.

She took a slingful for compass the day
she left to hunt a sky recognisably itself –

which would be north, she thought, across
the river. Sometimes when the wind changed

she could see it, almost, as through the eye of –

Exe

It takes shape sometimes, the idea of a river –
that is, the memory of it, and the places
it runs together: Topsham, Double Locks,

Countess Wear. Its potteries by the quay,
their *slips* and *vessels*, the men whose
tongues turned those terms as matter

of course. Its maritime museum: a name
and an echoing room of photographs,
behind glass, of the swan-shaped *Swan*

that was lost at sea by burning, leaving just
its dinghy *Cygnet* salvaged and roped off
on a plinth with white wooden plumage

so alien and inviting to the fingertips
the child that lies alongside to draw the ship
in flames in the air that billows dark above

the water has a feel for metamorphosis
without the word for it. Outside, the town
on its hills is roundabouts in palisades

of light blue railings, flood plains where men
plot the bed of the new canal and the shell
of a church, sandstone, open to the sky

to walk about in, whose plaque says *war*
and *destroyed by fire*. Outside, swans
double-cross their reflections on the river

running past the shed where earth's fired
to earthenware and on through the world
all around the page the child turns to mark

X for her place at the centre of things that are
beyond her and for the river that's somewhere
between its source and what it's the makings of.

Geography for Beginners

Is it a matter of landscape or language?
the book asks. Where would you most like to live:
mountains? flatlands? rolling hills and rivers?
The child strokes the illustrations, considers
from the vantage of her bed, in her purple-curtained room
how much she knows of the world –
her high garden and the sky that touches down
like a tent, on all sides. She senses the spring of grass
under her hand, the leaves of the book – open,
showing trees dwarfed by new-build and roads signed
in the foreign tongue that will be her fortune.
They invite the wind that translates as sticks and stones.
She is learning that words and things are cause and effect,
surely as the Christmas tree on the roof that stands for luck
will call down lightning through its cracked spine.
She is sitting upright in bed, holding the book. She knows
the truth of the question *how do you want to be?*
The words for it are over the hill and beyond.

The words for it are 'over the hill and – '. Beyond
the truth of the question, *how do you want to be,*
she is sitting upright in bed, holding the book she knows
will call down lightning through its cracked spine
surely as the Christmas tree on the roof that stands for luck.
She is learning that words and things are cause and effect:
they invite the wind that translates as sticks and stones
in the foreign tongue that will be her fortune.
Showing trees dwarfed by new-build and roads signed
under her hand, the leaves of the book open
like a tent on all sides. She senses the spring of grass,
her high garden and the sky that touches down –
how much she knows of the world.
From the vantage of her bed, in her purple-curtained room,
the child strokes the illustrations, considers
mountains, flatlands, rolling hills and rivers.
The book asks, where would you most like to live?
Is it a matter of landscape or language?

Song of Childhood

The off-beat chink of a cowbell.
Exeter, Gilgarran, Lodge Hill.

The eucalyptus and the Bramley,
the new red and gold Raleigh

bicycle in the butterfly bush,
the tooth I lost at Dawlish

past the spinning dinghies of Topsham
and the wind scutting across the Warren.

The far north was Cowley Bridge;
west, the soporific cows of Exwick

high above the tadpoles of Taddyford
and the sleeping dogs of Stoke Wood

proudly bore the name Friesian –
the liquorice stretch of the word on the tongue

like bootleg Allsorts eaten after dark
when figures went dancing in the carpet,

the walls said *this is the home service,*
the station said *this is Exeter St David's,*

and two by two the giddy cows and dogs
came out in between-time over Double Locks

to range the sky that was tall as a crane
all the way to Starcross, and back again.

Night Drive

You'll have been here before.
The flesh and blood of you, the bone

conducting your car down its own
tunnel vision. The road open, then shut.

Somewhere ahead white lines will lift
off into the sky's depth-charge as your radio

recites the constellations – *Dogger, Fisher* –

the way children down Taddyford, suggestible,
whispered toad-life into its cool brown stones.

In the valley the river echoed their soundings:
Old Match Factory, Quay and *Countess Wear*

where black swans feathered their reflections,
the ferryman chain-hauled passengers across.

Tonight the memory of it is buoyant as a boat
moored on the patch of sky in your headlights,

clear as the slip between a river and the name
for it: the echo of port in the night's starboard,

the *terra firma* that is silent in *Finisterre*.

Black Swans

(for my mother)

Because you say there were no swans
by Countess Wear, we can't have watched them

raised above eye-level where we stood on the path
and looking down on us as if we were the water

they trod in. Because there were none we
can't have seen the dark cropped fleur-de-lys

of their necks, the way they muscled in
on their own reflections, bill to red bill,

or the casual kick of one webbed foot,
the other a shadowy, upturned parasol.

The river was purely swanless; there was just
its feather-white torrent of water and a siren

pitched somewhere high above the town.
There were no cygnets; there was no argument

whether you can tell black from white, so young.
But do you remember how in the drought last year

a fisherman in waders forked the current? Now
do you remember the fluent, non-existent swans?

The Museum of Childhood

(for Lottie)

I

When you ask how I remember the past, as narrative
or snapshot, I think of your Pollock's-style perspective

box: the abrupt exits and entrances, the cardboard
scenery, small two-dimensional urns steadied

with a fingernail and the whole thing slightly
askew. How we each pressed an eye to the carpet

to take its measure and acclimatise to the colours
dashed in their inky outlines, their air of expectancy.

It was like that. Living outside and looking in
to England's conservatory of ghosts and geraniums

as through a window on a place with more rooms
than I'd words for in my first, diminishing language

I saw raw material. And all the time abroad grey
as the edges of the room where we straightened

unsteadily on our life-sized feet and blinked
at the awkwardly solid bookcase and bedhead,

where there was nothing to work with,
nothing to get a purchase on, where living

was practising ghostdom, the way we argued
whether it's the chair that passes through the hand

or the hand that passes through the chair.

II

The parts of your house were primary –
its porch, larder and scullery royal, crimson,

gold and indivisible as the slim stained
lights in the door, their cornered star.

The brass door-handles, string and bone carpet
and boxed-in stairs were the only stairs, carpet

and handles to fit those words. They were cagey
as crinolines, suggesting more than themselves.

And the back bedroom, the solid chill of it,
as if the house wrapped silence like the thing

a word stands unassumingly in place of.
The Grey Lady silhouetted against the window.

And the two of us, shadowing her.

III

What was it we were looking for when we lit out
through the French windows after dark in
our dressing-gowns and gave the name trap-door

to a Victorian manhole cover?
                                    The heavy ring to it,
as if the word could open a world.

What were we getting at, what were we using the real
things *for* when we climbed the wall
into the empty house next door,

made a study of two obsolete bicycles?

And what was it made us run the gauntlet of the iron-
jawed, finger-snatching postbox, or track the stream
through ferns in other people's gardens to the ford?

Everything we saw was sign and was the definite
article: the marble statue in its deep blue velvet
cushioned summerhouse, its ogre owner,

the largesse of the stream, coining light.

The Grey Lady solid and circumstantial
on a bicycle down by Clare Pike's house.

The dusk shaped like a bicycle, end-on.

What was it we were listening for when we went
up the bedroom stairs with palms pressed flat
against the dark –
                          metaphor before the word
metaphor, or our selves, the far side of the wall?

IV

If I give you this to read, will you say
I should tell how we ran off, aged four,

to paddle in Lily Brook in January?

How black chewing gum made us invisible,
how we flew with a tailwind and a parasol,

how you said we were in the novel of our lives
and I wrote stories where we all had pseudonyms?

Yesterday you sent an accidental voicemail
so there I was listening, half way up Ninetree Hill,

to the steam-iron sound of a printing press,
broken lines of a conversation in French.

And I thought of you telling the story to your daughter –
telling her all the stories, sketching in for her

something of the forms we fill. And of the word,
daughter: its promise and solidity, its dailiness.

And of a real errata slip: for *exits*, read *exist*.

V

This should be a conclusion – April,
thirty years on, Inez in a bundle
of clothes on your back.

We slip past the new-build, count
the steps down to the stream,
get the camera out.

This should be the full
circle, the final telling detail –
and so it is.

What to say of it?
We were here for a bit
and then we were cold

and on the bus back to Exeter.
But think of us dipping a toe
in the water, through and beside

those two girls, aged ten or so,
who are out posting a letter.
One in a hat and three jumpers,

the other with an umbrella.
The man walking his terrier
half-recognises them, half

swings his lead. He looks back,
sees they're still there. Sees
nothing out of the ordinary.

VI

Open the dark.
The step to the back bedroom creaks.

Open the dark door. You know
there's nothing there –

or nothing but boxes, crayons,
an ironing board.

The window is dark.
The sky is drawn in a slant

net curtain. The air
on the stairs is warm

by comparison, and shadows grow
full-skirted in the dark

by the window – at least dark
enough to imagine nothing

there, and the exact shape of it:
nothing but seeing through.

Revenant

I will go down by Jacob's Ladder
    by flip-flop, sea-salt and vanilla
I will go down by Taddyford
    by frogspawn and a hole in my boot
I will go down by the canal
    in my bridesmaid's shoes of white satin
I will go down by St Erth
    on a rope across the stream
I will go down by Dawlish
    by a stone's skimming quickstep
    by the ocean's erasures
And I will go down by Hope Cove
    by pitch and slipway, by pampas grass
I will go down by Princess Pavilion
    by grotto, night-light and sea-shell
I will go down by Budleigh Salterton
    by mud, moss, one-legged postbox
by Lily Brook and Little Knowle
    by water under the bridge
And I will go down by Cot Valley
    by wheelhouse, llama and camellia
    by lay-by where sleeping dogs lie
    by sea, by swing, by beginning
Where I will go down by Lodge Hill
    by elm, sledge and kaleidoscope
And I will go down by Gilgarran
    by sunset, cowbell, ice cream van
And I will go down by Gilgarran
    by myself, by name alone

Anecdote

Of course there was a house, but it wasn't *that*
important. Past the ring road and through a gap

in the wall it was the cemetery we went for –
a burial ground of grass overtopping its stony

non-conformist dead and the past that *hic iacet*,
sacred. It was summer then and silent. Only

the house was more so: boarded and ivy-leaved,
a three-storeyed volume of dark that we ignored.

What the policeman saw was two girls elaborate
with petticoats and parasols who ran the length

of the graveyard and vaulted into a 12-foot fall.
Then nothing. Some children in the park on swings.

The pale sun lapidary. The sheer height of the wall.
And this was over thirty years ago. It was nothing.

And the house had no bearing on it at all.

Forecast

Some day they'll stand here, the conservationists
of the future, small sable brushes pointilliste
in the dots and dashes of the walls. *Familiar,*

they'll call the outlines, with *a real resemblance.*
Isn't this the very house we're standing in?
And look, they had cats with collars, just like ours.

But the inscriptions puzzle. What does it mean
to say that horses fly in a half-forgotten language?
Will fossil-hunters find signs of equine cartilage

notched for wings? Or, if they went with the wind
casually as with carriage, how did we descend
from those leaps and bounds to our literal-minded

amazement, fingering a whittled length of bone
and feather in an abandoned attic and enquiring
dumbly, *how does this contraption go, again?*

Ferryman

The jokers say, you'll be for getting us across
by hook or by crook, but those aren't the words
for this crank, this pulley or wrench I chuck
and clamp, chuck and clamp to the chain that spans
the river. The name for it's nothing you'll need
to remember on our passage just half a hundred
yards upstream from the weir's sleek unravelling –
I don't think of it, your life and death in my hands,
or between them for that small space when I free
the pulley and what's holding the boat back from
the slipstream's beyond me – a catch in the laws
of time? It's as if she couldn't grasp her freedom.

I start before dawn. You are so many, uniform
as children, pale faces all eye, or do I mean
all soul, individual only in the passing gesture
of a hand I can barely identify in the half-light
about my feet: one idly trailing a second wake
back to the town we came from, others clasped –
not in prayer, I think, but eager for our landing
on the quay and dispersal to their apprenticeships
in silver, glass, and clay: each a visible way
of teaching fire its business of transformation.
The townspeople looking down from their hill
wonder at the small red wings that flicker indistinctly

behind the veil they call windows each time we lift
a melting globe of glass on its staff and quench it
in the river to make a vessel you could drink from,
cupping between your hands all you'll ever remember.

Child at a Museum

It's the eyes she notices, the bearded stag and boar
watching her darkly, in partial recognition.
It's the likeness and not the caption, *Forest Fire*,

though overhead the birds are winging it in all
directions and those human-hearted animals
lift their heads slow to scent the source of the danger.

The flame is floreate, burns discreetly off-centre.

We've seen it so often, that speaking picture:

the cattle's silent glossolalia, the dumb beasts
standing with their hearts in their mouths and little
people running about, wise after the horse. But its

sea and sky meet lightly still, as they always do –
as we might answer each other in a close-to-true
likeness or as, in a forest, four eyes touch and go.

Juxtaposition

As a child, *mezzanine* was a solid, barred
and angular in the palm of my hand.

A platform for viewing the real live dead
giraffe and mirror-length portrait of a lady

whose black and silver scarf unscrolled
in embroideries of *esprit d'escalier*.

I thought there were no pictures without words.

But today when that russet dog ran the length

of the island's grasses like the wind feathering
its backbone, *fleet* didn't begin – nor *flute*,

with the wind, over the hills and far.
But like the child in the vestibule spelling *O*

altitudo, like the question I meant to ask you –

Is it the real thing? Do you feel it too,
this sudden escalation, I mean this fall? –

yesterday, in passing on the stairs, it's gone.

Night-watch

Somewhere tonight is a frontier
between languages, our sentries darkly
passing watchwords, lip to lip.

Alongside the world is talking quietly
to itself about roadworks and batsmen
hanging on – *when Bridge Street's closed* –

upside down in Australia, its voices
spinning the curvature of the globe
while between us at our fingertips

the words *dear heart* and *welcome* pass
and pass again too quick for sense –
or is it nothing but, this limber

linguistic cat's cradle of mistaking
one tongue for another, as when *h* and *t*
are silent in my word in your ear?

Tremolo

(for Paul)

The world is everything that is not the case.
There are too many ways about it.

Take that house: white, turreted, standing
so roundly out on the cliff, day after day,

summer after summer, it was stability
made thatch and fortified, a perfect suppose:

embowered, we said, and sleeping beautifully
among briars and imagined marble fountains.

Contrariwise, it came and went with the sun,
was out of reach and inevitably too close

to the edge as a poem for what's vanished
or the vanished sense of things existing

in their places has too much grammar –
and this is not that poem. Between ourselves,

suppose no before or after. There's the house,
seamless on its cliff in Devon for just as long

as you keep reading, and then some: sealed
on its dominions of kitchen and porch and hall.

And here in the mindslip is the cracked lintel,
the walls riffling outward, the sun breezing in

to where someone might stand on its awkwardly
enjambed threshold and claim in view of the sky's

sudden excess lucidity that the two things are equal
and equally true – which is, and is not, impossible.

There's a road

that runs like a caption to the coast.
The land shows its workings, as we do.

Off Gurnard's Head, a herd of cows:
arrhythmic gait and tails' switchback

no oil painting.
Omissions. Two donkeys tethered

out of sight. Whatever we talked about,
it wasn't *that*. Parsimony, or was it

truth-telling, the painter's habit
of erasure? That, perhaps.

The problems of starting over.
From the boot, a smell of turps.

And the road, its ellipses
a half-remembered quotation.

How did it go again?
It should have been early,

but it was late, driving back,
we saw those cows on the verge

so singular and matter of fact:
tawny, Friesian, black and tawny

filing the brow of the hill along
the top of the windscreen

and into their yard, one by one,
that evening like every other

putting the action to the words
and coming home –

or so we said, driving on.

Natural History

There was a cave.

???

A tin chest, half-embedded.
Protruding, the spines of – a windlass?
Rotary.

Round the headland, ammonites – entailed
embryonic not-quite birds in the hand.

Near the cave, the form of a harbour.
A flux of stones that stopped the river's mouth.

There was a cliff-fall: soused red
sandstone tumbling slowly to its weight.
The cave was sealed off.

In its walls, the crass score-keeping:
Tracy 4 Ben, Trish is a slag.

In my grandparents' house, in water-colour:
Chit Rock before its rock-wreck and erasure
from the pools where we fished for limpets –

an oblique angle on the human perspective.

???

On terraces up by the beach huts were girls
and boys, grown ones, smoking at full stretch.

There was a low-key transistor.

There was the time they dived from the white
ladder the beach is named for, angled skyward
as if shoulders, ankles or wrists could feather –

then involved, shell-like, at the tipping point
ripping into the downdraft so fast *sgraffito*
was the sound for it and for the tiding over.

They surfaced impossibly far out –
not fish-tailed, nothing so relatable.

Sure of itself, the sea said *Ahhh, ssshhh.*

Like Truth

Verily, that contradiction in terms, is like the view
from Trencrom: its two distinct coastlines rimmed

in the iris of one horizon. North, Rorschach heads
of gorse, the sun, and a sky so absolutely blue

it's singing (or so I'd say) where a boy flies a kite
whose tail strings together three neat full stops

in complete ellipsis...
                        South, the mist's thin
as if a painter had worked her brushes out to let

canvas show through the long-drawn-out call-signs
of gulls, rising.
                Two outlooks, equally distinct

and distinctly apart: verily, like truth, we always
come down one side or the other, though that kite

overhead weaves from north to south so fluidly
it's like a cat crossing the hill without thought

of pleasing *you* – and like the cat, it's fabulous
(or so I'd say) and also – *verily* – absolutely true.

Translations

'There are very few poems here that take the form of anecdote.'

It's instructive, the way the poet sits down and writes
'we drove out along the coast road, *Bloodflowers*
on the iPod', and the way the early autumn leaves
were turning. That is, she writes: 'the scarlet leaves,
self-glossing, were turning one by one'. You had to be

there to hear us talking about life and its metamorphosis
into art, of course, and how Giles painted the front room
as violin and square piano in ink and wash, an empty
chair solidly inhabiting its shadow. How I've hung on
to the picture, though the piano got pinched, the violin

mistaken for cricket bat, and the artist died. The moral
here's the elephant, proverbial – but then we discovered
two black donkeys down a lane to the cliffs, and a third –
grey, blinkered – with instructions not to feed. There'd
also have been geese and herring up the garden path,

no doubt, if we'd not been distracted by that calf-sized
red setter that almost had your leg, full of itself as those
three pylons on the rim of a bare washed field quite
electric with connections – or so the poet writes, having
read just two days before in a centuries-old history

of the world how Queen Semyramys of Egypt crafted
several dozen fake elephants from the skins of oxen
stuffed with hay. The history was a translation, and it's
instructive to think how *that* poet sat over it one day when
the hedges were a blaze of crimson foliage and out on

the coast road his neighbour's cows were kicking up
a dustcloud dense as the smoke there's no fire without
even as he wrote how eye-witnesses saw *the naturall
oliphauntes renne sturdily upon those ymagynatyve
monsters*, in a turn of phrase that simply says it all.

My Grandmother's Mirrors

She makes two of them, one small, one medium:
green glass in embossed pewter frames round
as portholes giving on a sea that see-saws

woodenly, islands hinging in and out of sight.
Her mind is off somewhere between the trees
of its own interior. Her medium is plaster.

In a year or so she'll discover clay: palms
extemporising the spinning third dimension.
These hard-pressed forms are interim.

Her hands cast darkly for their trefoil leaves.
Her children have long left home.
Holding the mirrors up to them, she holds

her face between her hands in the forest
she's twice moulded as a wreath of leaves.
The world repeats in its own medium.

In a year or so she'll discover clay.

Troy

Bridleless, and papier-mâché white
as the ridden snow – that is, grey –
one story would be how this idea

of a horse was collaged piece by piece
to something almost life-sized,
almost live, as if its maker had stopped

short only of breathing into those wide
open nostrils, cutting loose the hooves
from the rockers that hold it up, and down.

By T. Irving Pugh, out of Harrogate,
pre-war – that is, before the *first* war –
its almost intelligent, almost amber

eyes have reflected flames of nursery
fires and candles, the bars of grates
and window grilles and all the miles

it's gone through imagined forests
of oak and elm whose branches white
as the petticoats of its small, bookish

rider led the way with the night light
shining errant down the years that stretch
from Yorkshire to Chipping Norton –

where the story is how we drew it home
silently over snowy roads, off-white on
white, a great sleigh rocking slightly

on its runners, and how in its shy
sidelong movement I saw that other horse,
Casablanca, early evenings outside

my grandmother's house, shifting pale
and evanescent on the edge of what
we called the forest – until later,

in darkness, his hooves' cobbled echo
rang solid down the avenue the length
of the bedroom where we as children lay

not quite sleeping, eyes tightly closed
to the trees between its four white walls
and on the very edge of the known.

Gone to Ground

Say *unwalled* and what arises is rough grey stone –
the way the carapace of a fishing-boat, upturned,
invokes all the resemblances between sky and sea:
clouds drifting across the shell of the inverted
world that's unfamiliar, uncanny because it's known

and not known. The mind, literal and persistent
as the roots of a nameless grey plant (*honesty?*)
works its passage through the debris of what once
stood as a boundary and out into the cliff's thickets
of gorse and bracken. That is: the mind, nondescript

as the foliage of sea-pinks (thrift) or lichen,
but none of them, goes underground like the signs
of life we've imagined in the house we've yet
to enter, whose flower beds edged with granite
are home to abandoned snail shells in abundance

and there's no telling what's below in a garden
where the boat, righted, would make a planter
and the wall's standing stones a perfect support
for raspberries – where the word *unfallen* (unspoken)
means less *before*, more *put back together again*.

This low tide

the ebb's crepuscular and faintly
        reptilian – no,

those are not the words, though
the sounds are sufficiently
        scaly and very old.

The water's edge is limpid and soft-
pawed, soft-tongued, lapping
        and overlapping the sand

that's agglomerate iridescences
and that's a bed for amber,
        sea-green and translucent

glass – lager, chardonnay and milk,
as was. The embossing's blunt,
        obliterate – but

we'll pocket it, imagine it set in silver.
Precious, we say the sea says,
        taking its shells

for ear-drops. *Precioussss.*
And then – there's this
        solid x-ray

of a fish, or washed-up fish
negative: a full scale of vertebrae
    that begs the body,

the muscular rope of it, that runs
up to the skull's narrow ridgeplate
        with its lights punched

into enormous holes for seeing
through as in a ruined *library*
     we say irrelevantly

or (better) abandoned engine-house
where we sit bone-dry, looking out
     at small figures

crossing our sockets under a high
thin draft of the skyline. Staggered,
     they stoop occasionally,

one of them reaching through the absent
head for a rare shard of cobalt
     that's caught her eye.

The Weather in St Just

Rain and shine both walk on water
or on the rising tide of cloud that levels
with the cliff. Land here's mostly

on the receiving end. On my phone
the symbol for weather is only ever
wind – a scroll endlessly

wrapped up in itself – though inland
signs on its screen twin with signs
in the sky in duplicates

of sun, perfect parallax of rain.
We forecast by the flight-paths
of leggy little planes

that motor in from offshore, by how
night is a wrap or night is the stars
of ships out at sea

flowing seamlessly into the lesser sea
of lights that is the town. Either way,
the wind's insomniac

talking over us in elemental
                                  animadversions
fretting the knot in
                        the sting of the riddle
of its own tail
               liminal
                     worrier

of thresholds
            it sings
                       to the ear

unfurl

      to the heart

             open

               to the mind

just how far have you come?

Listen. What was the question?

               To the mind

at the core of its small granite house

                there is

no question

      but responses repeating

the unrepeatable

         present

               continuous

The Nightships

pass in twos and threes, intently heading north
in a concatenation of portholes, lightboxes

of their cargo on hold, or as single stars reflected
in the arc of the sky that encompasses them

whose look-outs looking out indirectly sight
land as an invasion of nightlights, an information –

as in mist lightships sound a bullish refrain
and shapes that pass are constellations in name alone

(the great seal and the lesser, the whale and moon-
calf in spindrift round each engine house whose

pilots are swayed by the sea's incantation
and the tide's turned tables, so all souls aboard

wake to a port and starboard indifferently the same
and themselves in cabins invisibly heading south again).

At Sea

As if they were barometers we check each morning
and say 'the Scillies are out', or not, taking note

in which of their many formations: a swell in
the contour-line where sea meets sky or peaks

of thundercloud just tipping the horizon.
Some days a pure idea of island, others

with a fine white band that must be beaches
where at night the coupled lighthouses reliably

two-time, two-time.
                    Last night I dreamed
we were linked by transepts: windblown ruins

arching westwards, the sun patched through,
and in the cove a cluster of rowing boats just

setting out, my dead husband steady in the bows
of the last of them, stretching me his hand –

Last night I woke to a moonpath, liquid light,
and all the gables down the hill in white-out.

My brother brought home photographs, said
the gardens were beautiful, but for all that

communication and the planes that belly in
on the hour with their engine noise on tow

I wouldn't go there, wouldn't want to know
that they inhabit their bodies just as we do

and looking daily at the view of sky ebbing
uninterrupted into tide say indifferently

'the coast is out', or 'lost', and run through
their fingers their imaginary beaches' mica.

Thesaurus

(for Jeffrey)

> Idle as a painted ship. Upon a painted ocean.
>
> S.T. COLERIDGE

As you say, idle isn't lazy, but still
as the sea, those dog days round the equator
when a ship is not a sail.

It's the senses lapped like shipboard,
the ship lapping the void that is itself,
all at sea: which is to say, groundless.

And it's the sailors, not engaged in work,
but light-headed, out of their minds, or delirious.
It's the albatross, out of circulation.

Think of the word as medium – a blue-
green transparency leading down and down
to no solid result. Of the mind in its quick

brown study probing the depths
like a painter's brush or the fox that jumps
out of the blue from quay to shipboard.

A fox? you ask. Where did that spring from?
Oh, I say, it was there in the beginning.
As idle is the ocean it is hair of the dog.

Anonymous

is the poet behind the lines of the western wind
whose lampblack blots the veined vellum margins
in hands and characters that are not her own.

Is the wind that loops its long cursive through the grass,
and the artist who types on a paper-white screen
I hid, sometimes in plain sight, a dozen silver ladders.

Is the ladder grafted in the fork of an apple
or – at a loose end – propping the garden wall:
a fantasia on initial H whose cornucopia of fruit,

roses and songbirds extends the length of the gutter.
Is the sea the heavier by a pocket-sized ladder,
the drop in the ocean that's the small weight of the rain.

Like the borrowed tongue (*Christ that my love –*)
and the artist's manifesto posted in plain sight
(*it wasn't important to me they should be seen*),

it's what's at hand. That is: like the ladder's missing
third dimension, like the wind and its entail riffing
the field in those serial doppelgängers – *cc, pp, ff* –

that are blown through, and blowing away. Like this.

Riddle

(for Ian)

I'm princely support on a bad hair day,
a riff on an angelic scale. A way

of putting two and two and four together
like the shaft of the apple cart,

preposterous, that comes before the horse.
A shaky platform for lightbulb jokes

and direct line to the gods: what comes
and goes around in the clammy palms

of a stagehand. A working definition
of recalcitrance, the outer limit of paint –

or, in extended use, a sign of aspiration.
I'm also a cinch, a black cat's temptation,

a business-like substitute for the serpent
and all-too-human ribcage without the heart

though I'll frame for you a series of stills
of your world in descending order: spills

of wood splintering from a fascia board, an apple
laddered green on red, that black cat with tail

plumed high measuring its retreat. For as long
as you hold me I'm what keeps you looking

in from outside. And I'm a tippling probe
for the sky, an awkward extension of the globe

where you stand grounded and angling – for what,
you ask: Is it this? Perhaps not quite, not yet.

Losing It

Like anaphora, the figure of a stream
and a man who stands, one leg either
side of the water, holding a jar.

Like the jar he passes smoothly from shore
to shore, its belly full of standing water:
a jar with two handles, like a door.

Like china that just comes apart
in your hand, splitting the blue and white
figures that pause as they cross the water.

Like the broken man still gripping
the disjointed handles and the smooth-
bellied body of water that flows between —

Write it down, he says, so I can grasp
the word for the thing I've lost, which is
like — something. Amphora. Carrying across.

What the poet is trying to say is

not paraphrase. There's the word, the wood,
the world and the sun's irregular interstices

between the trees ablaze like the white wall
of a house marking the path as ink makes

signs for door and window and for the terms
we attach to them: *threshold*, *hope*, or *loss*.

As for arrival and departure, they're a given:
that's just life, as anyone can tell. Conversely,

what the poet is trying to say is the progress
through the wood of the word, blindly

inching out its roots and branches. Is
what it is to be in the thick of the self's

slow-leaved metamorphosis, its bifurcations,
the heart's expanding and contracting rings.

To paraphrase, what the poet is trying to say
is just the material we have to work with.

In the thick of the world between the wood
and the word, what the poet is trying to say is.

Lifelines

Some say, around the headland's the point
you'll want to stop and look back the way
you came, see those cormorant-shouldered

rocks that mark the cove you started from
with eyes the summer visitors bring to seals:
bifocal, and endlessly willing to believe.

That, they say, is the point, though others swear
the days just come and go and any fishbone
or bladderwrack they wash up is nothing but

pieces of string too short to save. One minute
a pigeon's self-importantly fluffed among
gulls in the harbour, the next it's gone again.

Myself, I couldn't tell from one wing-beat
to the next how I got here, only how flight
repeats, though I understand the small stone

towns I pass are settlements, and sometimes
in the folds of coastline my shadow smokes
like goose or angel a house shows white as

the fly-leaf of a book I found once, secondhand,
whose inscription was in writing I used to know
so well I could trace the flow of it, its characters

in the making: the enclosed spaces at their centres
integral as skeleton to fish or fish to bird's eye
in the current towing the sea's quick hieroglyphs.

Five-finger Exercise

Like the wind that hymns the fence's two barbed wires,
the tide that flexes the intervals between its high
        point and its low,
the tall striped lighthouse that calls time, time, time,
        the painter has his idiom:

his telegraph poles, rooflines and long arm of horizon,
his small-leaved evergreens, chimney pots and tides
        that come and go.
Startling, a rook blacks out the lighthouse and two dormers:
        he'll get that down tomorrow

like the unlikeness between the wires and their singing,
the chimneys with and without smoke, the lives of things
        and the forms of them
which he'll repeat as the tree in the foreground
        keeps growing out of itself,

as beyond the blot of the rook the lighthouse signals on.

Still Here

(after Naomi Frears)

The way your films show it, simply
to exist isn't simple, but a form of sight
reading, reading across, reading in –

difficult as watching two distinct
scenes at once: here a parasol neatly
triangulates itself, there a landscape

runs blindly past the emergency exit.
And was that lightning? Twice?
It wasn't the same.
                              Outside in January

a frame of railings holds the tide – once,
again; inside, the film of water's still
July in its intricacies, its dark and light.

And between's the business of Saturday:
skateboarding, shopping, promenading
people with three hands full and dogs

whistling along to Newlyn –
                              cut here
or there
          it all adds up to something
like balance, equivalence, taking in

what's there to be seen. This porch light
in a storm, its shaky arrhythmia.
That stone stretch of house shot low,

sideways on, with cars passing, passing
like clock – no, like metronome against
the small human movement of the lens

and this pond dark under its open-palmed
statue and raft of leaves mirroring that other
half-remembered pond dark under moss

and rhododendron at the top of the garden
and so unutterably still the child, disquieted,
turns back to the house and doesn't mention it.

When we say stories are worth telling,
don't we mean the interstices?
                              In St Just
this morning, in fog, the world was down
to incidentals: brake light, bush, black dog
somewhere between discovery and erasure –

or erasure and discovery, different again –

as when two people leave the gallery, walking
slowly along the uncut exposure of the bay,
and one claims 'I want to write about silence',

and we remember this, among other things –

like fog on a roll, a film's white noise
before the pictures come in or words
reprise how it was in the beginning –

and like a sheet of paper before a mark is made
it is – and isn't – wholly what she meant to say.

The Pond

Undivined, a double cube of water.

A surface of solid peridots lying
out of mind in the shrubbery for years.

A thought, pre-verbal. Or, adjectival:
sinister, umbrageous, amphibian.

The pool, the missing substantive.

Memory, like earth, encapsulating
something other than itself.

That long-haired, long-legged child tumbling
unlooked-for down the hill and calling from far
outside earshot how we'd never believe –

The gravel sparking from her feet.

At the height of the garden, the mass of it.

The rhododendrons hushed and lustrous.

The convex steps down. Concrete.
What we didn't know we had always known.

The fluted artifice of its edges, its urns.

Treehouse

New Year's Eve, we walk the path along
the edge of things, feet at burial height,
eyes level with the rimed grasses.

Puddles are long knives, mirror shards,
each berry bezelled in a crown of thorns,
and the church is down on its haunches.

Behind, our years of pausing at this turn,
the way the sea's a known quantity
that pulls its weight out of mind.

But today, differently, a treehouse –
or its makings: a rig of planks and batten
for lintel. A space outlined in air –

or platform to sit and look down on the ground
we look up from, imagining the view:

the fine-toothed frost-bitten fields climbing
to the treeline where rooks cluster in
off-beat musical notation. Beyond them,

the sea, still out of sight. Here, at the tree's
foot, black-booted, we provide the human
scale: typecast figures small, convenient,

and fictional. We were never there.
The treehouse, though, is real. Its apertures,
its well-defined void and surprisingly solid floor.

Sneyd Park Sketchbook

> If the place I write from is real, then I must be allegorical.
>
> W.S. GRAHAM

I *Self-Portrait with River*

Suppose you lived here, what language would you choose
for the broad brush of river, the towpath and silver-
skinned estuary? For the small foreign mountains,
the silk skein of river, copper-beech-coloured beach,
or the grey-green floodplain and neat brick houses?

Pigeons tumble to the window. Cows graze on the knoll.
In the mirror's Australia ebb and flow reverse:
flow and ebb again. Even the sky is tidal.
The port holds the river on the tip of its tongue.
Suppose you lived here, how would you name

the shipyards, the cars on the motorway, the wind
spooled through the wind-farm? In view of the river's
double-tongued tongue-twist, how would you explain
the scales tipping between *is* and *said-so* or the balance
of life your reflection gives you for your own?

All this went unnoticed for centuries:
the river's casual tiding to and fro,
the sea's fingerhold, the naive cows
grazing this or that side of the knoll
the river's ups and downs
the river making its bed
the cows *au naturel* in beige and brown

when someone built a house for the view
and between its glazing bars the self-
divided cows walked in twos and threes
and the sun set through the beeches
where the river lay low, the river
flooded like silver nitrate
preparing the ground for later when

someone sold the plot for estate,
fly-over and rugby pitch, for wind
turbines keeping time and time again,
though the fog still obliterates the river
the river rises through the fog
the periodic cows come and go
and in the turret of the sub-divided

house a tri-partite mirror shows
how the middle ground recedes, the cows
quite naturally multiply and the Avon
doubles up on itself, running its course
so long, so long between Severn and Severn,
between the sky and its ink-dark carbon,
here you couldn't only once think of home.

III *Self-Portrait as Lady of Shalott*

She knows the edges are important.
There's no picture without a frame.
The river's movement is vertical (in or out).
The wind lifts the skylight again and again.

Off beyond the headland a single turbine
ticks over and over, marking time.
Off beyond the headland, the Severn,
Cardiff. Her flat is in suspension

between bridge and bridge – that is,
between the sea, the river and its clearly
transparent name. The waves are backing
and re-backing, the wind is spooled

and stored, like twine. On the towpath
a small figure in red shoulders its whole
belonging as it makes for the coast
that's the vanishing point between sea and sky.

Or so she says, reading between the lines.

IV *Self-Portrait from Memory*

It's hard to say what this is, exactly.
Suppose a woman receding. The habitual arc of the street.
Suppose you have seen this before. Suppose a woman reading.

In Sneyd Park, a carved bird balanced on a painted cage.
In Stockbridge, a white bird. A collaged page.
Through the bars, the sky's tissue torn by beech trees.

Through the bird, the sea. Listen, the leaves are turning.
Listen, this is the truth of the matter: at least six things
at a time. The other sound you're hearing's that small

grey cat, slipper on the stairs at the back of the mind.

V *Self-Portrait from Life*

Behind the poem, the poem.
The mind, cat-like, nosing the gap between the words
and the thing it speaks of.

Behind the life, the life.
The cat (smoky, mackerel-backed) off about its business,
as beyond the Severn, Wales,

as between here and there the sea
there's no getting across, though swifts through the glass
come close to reflecting on it: migrant, tined

tails facing both ways, and audibly comparing notes.
The word is, things might have been different –
as at dusk, when all the riding lights of Newport

come out, behind the world's a world
where rivers run uphill and that moonshine crescent
in the Avon's a boat homing on the wind

which, in other words, I've whistled up for you.

An Unwritten Novel

There would be children, three of them.
Long-grassed gardens spilling to the river.
A piano playing the next door down but one.

There would be children, three of them –
Orfee, Ichys, Perdita, or Ellie, James, and John –
their voices in the orchard crying Styx for Avon

while urban foxes make recycling their own.
The parents are distracted. They take a lodger
whose window, nights, lights up like a quotation.

The woman opposite keeps a ledger of every
time the children call her witch for neighbour,
and how Montpelier, nights, is walking streets

of shadows. She knows the man who left so late
was not the lodger, how the child that's missing
came from south of the river, where windows,

nights, frame lives like eye-rhymes for our own.
They say that nothing we've begun is irreversible.

There'd be children, two of them, and a woman

writing how the lost child's hand lay in mine
lightly as a bird and with a bird's fine bones.

And distantly, across the water, that piano tune.

Still Life

Artless on the table, three narcissi.
The gap between one petal
and the next, unfurling.

Light's lip on the rim of a jug.
The time it took to get there.
The time it took to lay it on.

The weight of what's brought to bear.
No sun.
Behind the glass, a sudden

movement of doves passing.
                              Doves?
Their breasts salmon, their fanned
tails copper verdigris.

The canvas, as before.

Snapshot of a Marriage

Returning late, he sees her silhouetted
in the landing window, an awkward
pietà with duvet that fills the frame.

By day she knows the measure of the boards
she treads; by night she dreams new storeys,
stairs that rise to meet her.

At his fold-out desk he draws the house
turreted. She can see herself in it, knows
he'd lift her across the threshold

if she'd only trust as a sleepwalker does
the candle she cups blindly, caught
light-fingered in its living flame.

Instead of a Mirror

It was never a good mirror, if a good mirror
gives a good likeness: in its green shade faces
came and went hazily as if underwater, rippling
through a corner of sky, a branch and jackdaw.

It was never a good mirror, but for twenty years
or more it held and even when last night its several
stone weight came down in darkness with just a trail
of gold and plastered horsehair, a quarter inch dent

in the floor as witness of its final double somersault
the glass lay intact and still showing that same square
of blue as if there were no unbreakable chain of cause
and effect, or as if the wind had changed when it fell.

And because it was not a good mirror the wall
looks much the same now under its replacement
print where half-reflected faces flit against the tall
white façade of a house in Kingsdown, its purple

door inviting your glance casually to explore a hall
whose chessboard diagonals anchor the interior
volumes of stairwell and landing that lead round
to a balcony where the framed view's familiar

as the room you've slept in for decades now or
the bed's iron railings firm in your grasp under
the plane tree and that bird in its angular patch
of sky indeterminately homing or taking flight.

Domestic Science

When they moved to the high-rise, the children came quickly –
small, speechless, as if they'd always been there.

The white cloud at the window was striped with railings.
She set out pots of beans in rows,

watered the compact earth. The children grew
tall and pale and *stilted*, she thought, their loose

limbs stringed. She bought a rabbit, fenced a corner
of the kitchen for it. She bought a dog or two.

The straw walked. The bean stalks grew. The children
came and went. The days put out runners, sported years.

She remembered there were words for this – *her tether*,
and *the roof*. She side-stepped. She bought an aviary,

hung it like a second skin in the single bedroom: cagey,
elastic and tremulous. The children demanded finches.

She told them how she'd cut a door to match the door,
how she'd step inside, just for a minute.

She told them there were no two ways about it.

Spital Square

(for George & Clarissa)

She doesn't know yet what she's doing here,
but she's dressed for it in black with purple
curtain-fabric patches on her duffle bag.
Her scarf's cerulean to the sky's shot silk.
She is standing in the middle of the square

naming the parts of the houses – *fanlight*,
portico – like a child curating its small possessions.
She notes *embrasures of rusticated coade stone.*
She also remembers the boat that brought her here,
the great illuminated globes of Liverpool Street

overhead in the domed dark where footsteps
without visible feet sounded on metal walkways.
She's not an architect yet, she's not anything,
but yesterday when she read how an eighteenth
century tourist wrote of London's terraces

they give the idea of cages with sticks and birds,
she sensed the shape of things she wants to communicate.
The spire reflected in the weavers' clerestories: *that*
comes into it, and the clouds' scribbled annotations –
their almost legible graphs for *dormer, sky, light.*

Object Lesson

Sunday morning and a train cuts slowly through the skyline
like a ship pulling out of harbour between crazily paved
rooftops and aerials and laundry's limp semaphore across

a window where someone holds two halves of a plate
like an archaeologist finding out sequence, or lifts
her pearls as if each formed an elliptical opening on the world.

She looks like the photo a woman might have shown
to her children, captioned 'my mother before I was born'.
The pearls, their milk-white reflection.
She must already be someone's daughter.

But this morning she's alone in her room with the sky
and its squat church at anchor, with the train passing through.
She thinks there's something she might make of it.
It must be going somewhere. It looks emblematic.

By now, it will have got to Canterbury years ago.

Initialisation

(for John)

When all poems' lines began with capital initials
Houses had roots that ran down into the ground.
The rooms of the houses were the mind's interiors
Whose fingers walked them like a compositor's
Seeing feelingly the type tray's upper and lower
Orders, separating *h* from *o* and murmuring
Over the dark matter of the open spaces: *mmmn*.

When all poems' lines began with capital initials
There were no orphans and widow was erratum
For window, or windows: square, self-justifying,
Perfectly aligned. Each showed a landscape
And its familiars of off-white house, cliff,
Estuary: the mind's furniture that's configured
And reconfigured each time the poet who inhabits

The A-framed attic of the house with its view
Of a dinghy bravely bent on the horizon writes
A poem whose lines all begin with capital initials
And each initial forms an aperture on a world
In miniature whose immaculate gilt sun
Illuminates the house, the boat, the open spaces
Of the ocean O without end before the fall.

The Question of Things Not Happening

Sometimes nothing gives.
Your smile, an open invitation
that led to nothing in particular.
The dead letters piled on the carpet.
The twice-daily grind of the door.

Sometimes the signs are against us.
Detour. Delays possible till August.
Sometimes there are no signs –
just a black spin where the road
elides to ice, an obdurate stone wall.

And then, above the ploughed field,
birdsong. A weak sun. All calm
as if the girl might step unharmed
from her crumpled body in a world
where life carries on, like before.